ONLINE REPUTATION MANAGEMENT & REVERSE SEO

How to enhance and defend your online reputation in 30 hours

KOZ KHOSRAVANI

KozWealthSystems.com   Copyright 2015   Koz Khosravani

ONLINE REPUTATION MANAGEMENT & REVERSE SEO

How to enhance and defend your online reputation in 3o hours

Donald Trump's former online marketing and business coaching guru, and former Harvard & UCLA teaching fellow and lecturer, Koz Khosravani, teaches the secrets of applied online reputation management. Learn to monitor, claim, enhance, and repair your online reputation. Don't allow your enemies and competitors destroy your good name, Your personal and business success depends on it!

KOZ KHOSRAVANI

So, what is the title of this mini book all about? Online Reputation Management and Reverse SEO? Well, your online reputation can suffer on 2 broad areas: social media and search engines. In fact these days, anyone who wants to do business with you (or even date) will "Google" you!

In the field of search engine optimization (SEO), we focus on 1 website and try to bring it to the top area of the top page of Google (and even Yahoo and Bing). The process of online reputation management (ORM) is in reverse! That is, the targeted website has negative information about you so instead of taking it to the top page, we want to delete it if possible, and if not, push it to lower pages of search results.

By pushing it lower, in plain English, we create many other mini sites and push them above the site with negative information. So the idea is to create sites under our control with positive information about you and then get them ranked as high as possible (hoping that their ranks will go above the site with negative information). The theory being is that people only look at the top page of Google and very few people will look at page 2 or lower. Hence, the name of this mini book that has the words "reverse SEO"!

Ok, let's begin!

Companies that do not take advantage of online marketing and search engines lose the potential for significant profit. Up to 45 percent of online transactions started with the use of a search engine. Most potential consumers only scan the first couple of links of a search engine meaning companies need to have their company searchable and prominent.

Not only that but all web presence leaves a trail. With potential customers only scrolling through a couple search engine links, it is vital for companies to make sure the links that come up for their company show favorable information.

Often websites such as yelp, where commentators can review various companies, will be some of the first to come up. Companies need to keep track of their image on these reviewing platforms to make sure they project a positive image. If negative reviews do emerge, companies should address these comments directly opening a channel for conversation with the upset party. This will show other potential customers that the company cares about their image and the happiness of their customers.

You see, your online brand has an effect on your online reputation and vice versa!

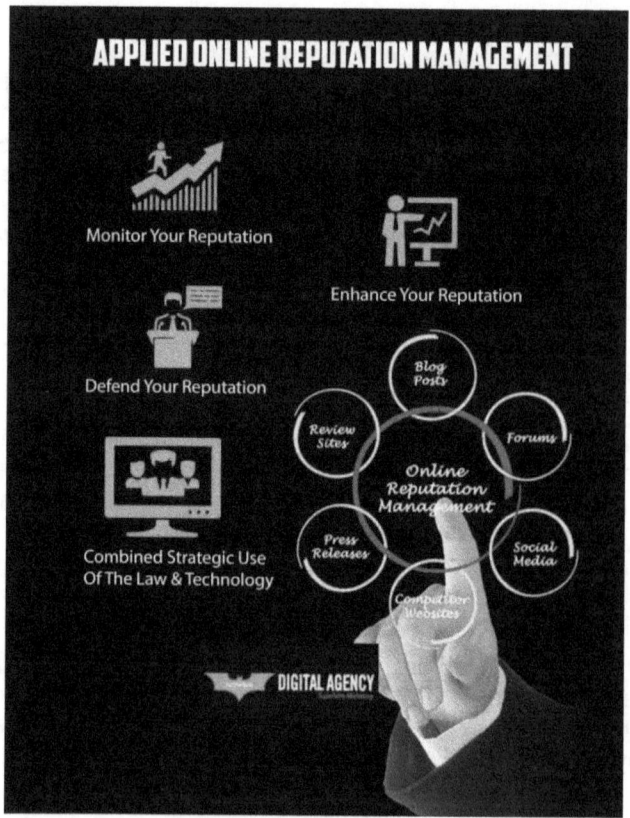

Cyber-bullying and reputation attacks on teens, families and businesses!

Your teenage daughter receives an anonymous email from someone containing hateful language that brings her to tears (or worse, potential thought of suicide). Your younger son gets bullied online by bunch of technology-savvy schoolmates who make life miserable for him. Your husband's firm dives into bankruptcy due to an online reputation attack by ruthless competitors or even anonymous jealous 'friends' behind his back; his relations with you deteriorate and affect your personal lives!

What do all these cases have in common? The answer is the use of the internet to attack your character, business, and life. While the rate of the attacks online is increasing, cyber laws are progressing too slowly to respond to the ever-changing world of internet. You need help to protect your family!

Luckily, it is quite possible to build an online reputation barrier to shield you from such attacks. It takes going through 4 steps outlined below:

Dealing with psychological and emotional hurt: Understand that many people are attacked online every day. You are not alone! It is important to remember that these attacks are malicious but almost never have any factual basis, so don't let them get to you! Remember that you have the power and access to tools to fight back.

Monitor your online reputation on search engines and social sites: You should check the top 3 pages of search engines such as Google, and look for anything negative about your family or your firm. You can use online tools such as Google alerts to be notified of anything said about you online and decide to get such alerts routinely.

Check all your social media sites such as Facebook to see what is being said about you. To make life easier for yourself, use online tools such as socialmention.com that will monitor any keywords including your name.

Claim and increase the virtual real estate about your family online: Purchase various domain names containing your name such as JohnDoe.com, JohnDoe.Org, etc. You will need these domain names to represent many mini sites and blogs built for your online brand and reputation. Then, use some of the free sites such as sites.Google.com, blogger.com, wix.com, weebly.com and WordPress.com to showcase positive information about you (or your children) with appropriate pictures. The site content can be family-oriented facts, biographies or anything else that you feel is positive in nature and builds your brand.

Once you have set up these domain names and websites, when someone uses a browser and types for example JohnDoe.Info, they will see the positive site you created. Even if you don't want to link the domain names to the sites, as long as the sites you created use your name as part of the original site (http://Sites.Google.com), you will get noticed by search engines. An example of one of the many free sites I personally have that still maintains search engine exposure is: https://sites.google.com/site/kozkhosravanibio.

You want to expand your virtual real estate beyond creating

websites, into the realm of the social media landscape. Take time and create great profiles, including your name, pictures and other relevant and positive information to major social sites such as Facebook, Twitter, LinkedIn, YouTube, Pinterest, Instagram and others. These sites are ranked very high on search engines so your profiles on them will rate highly as well.

Now you might be intimidated and not sure how to manage all these new sites, simply adding your basic information, biography, fun facts and pictures once is great start. To get them ranked even higher, you must add weekly content to them. Thankfully, there are tools such as Hootsuite and WordPress that you can use to link to other social sites you own, so by writing a blog post once, you can, in effect, have the same article automatically posted on Facebook, Twitter and many other social sites! Let machines fight for your family's reputation and not just you!

Neutralize the negative attacks: The final step to protecting yourself is by neutralizing, or even having certain sites deleted from search results through the rule of law as well as through negotiations! If you need a quick way to deal with damaging information, you can hire an attorney who specializes in virtual slander.

In some cases an attorney can gain a court order to find your attackers and sue them. Your hired attorney may also negotiate with the webmaster of various sites to directly eliminate the negative information.

While we are showing you how to take care of your online reputation needs yourself, there are in fact, times when you can benefit from having an experienced anti-slander attorney on your side! But again, don't go with just any attorney. They MUST specialize on online reputation defense and slander!

Law Firms Providing Brand & Online Reputation Defense

Law Firm Online Reputation Management Services

01 Reputation Analysis

Reputation Enhancement 02

03 Reputation Defense

Only Law Firms Can Sue Online Attackers For Slander

04

Corporate Online Reputation Management For When Your Company is on the Hitlist

Today if you apply for a job, there are very few instances where interviewers ask for references - they simply turn to Google to get the answers they need. The Internet has become part of people's daily existence, and it is the most revolutionary medium for communication ever experienced. Individuals and businesses are using the Internet for information and communication and nothing holds them back to vent their feelings for the world to see.

No longer is corporate online reputation management only associated with big brands. Even individuals and small businesses are targeted with venomous comment that can put them out of business permanently. There was a time before the Internet came about, when complaining about services or products was never done publicly.

Not only that, companies didn't engage with their customers the way they do today and customers played a passive role too, never daring to voice their feelings in a powerful way. Bad publicity and putting a company or brand in the limelight for all the wrong reasons has become commonplace and can spell disaster for a business.

Improving your Online Reputation

Corporate online reputation management services are becoming highly sought after in order to help businesses maintain a positive on-line presence. Today anyone can say anything about anybody online. Social media has meant that consumers can have an enormous audience with whom they can vent their anger and share all their grievances with. Consumers are passing comments about you and your brand via different online platforms. These platforms are -

■blogs and forums
■social networking sites such as LinkedIn, Facebook and Twitter
■review sites
■information and resource sharing sites

There are actually very few laws in place to regulate what is posted online. It is mind boggling to contemplate that Yelp, which is a leading ratings and review site is visited by no less than 40 million consumers during the month, and that customers are looking at some 14 million submitted reviews.

Imagine the extent of the damage done to your company if a disgruntled employee had to place negative images or comments on this particular review site? Just one negative review can dissuade many future would-be prospects from ever being interested in your products or services.

Sales can be Negatively Affected because of Derogatory Tweets

When people look up a business online, with corporate online reputation management services, people will only find positive information. Today the Internet has changed everything, and people are jumping onto social media and tweeting about products, services and even certain people.

There are some marketing executives who fail the company's they are representing simply because they don't grasp that without online reputation management, the company's sales can be damaged if these comments are negative.

Shareholders for instance are known to research an executive's reputation before investing in a company, and certainly celebrities do that before endorsing a company's products. Executives' reputations can certainly affect the kind of press the company gets.

Damage Control becoming Increasingly Difficult

Corporate online reputation management has a huge impact on a company's revenue, and marketing executives need to be protecting their company's good image online. It will be difficult and costly to restore a company's reputation after negative comments online.

With the rise in the use of social media, as well as the popularity of user-generated review sites such as Yelp, managing your online reputation has become critically important. It is the sheer number of voices involved on social media, continuously voicing their complaints and giving negative feedback which has made damage control so difficult.

No wonder online reputation management (ORM) services are so important for putting a halt on negativity aimed at your brand.

Stop Negative Comments Spreading like Wildfire

Of course the first step in social media reputation management is knowing what's being said about your business in the first place. You need to actually identify those keyword and hashtags related to your brand so as to monitor conversations that are taking place on social networking sites.

There are tools such as Hastagify.me and SocialMention for

instance which can be used to monitor these keywords. These tools allow you to search social networks for keywords and hashtags related to your business. With Google Alerts, which is free, you'll receive regular notifications as soon as your brand is mentioned. Once you know what is being said about your brand online, you can respond quickly and appropriately before the negative comments spread like wildfire.

Before you contact an ORM company, first consider your goals before hiring a reputation management company to restore and protect your brand's on-line presence. Some of the main roles to look for when choosing an ORM service will be -

■**Content development and management** - to rank well in search engines and to build up a good reputation, you need quality content which is organized, relevant and well written. It will also require quality press releases so as to broadcast word about your business in the right manner. This way Internet users will find positive results about your business which will add credibility to your brand.
■**Social media management** - companies make full use of- and benefit from social media networks such as Facebook, LinkedIn, Google+, SlideShare, YouTube, Twitter and Pinterest. However a horrendous image or comment can have a lasting detrimental effect on your business and ORM services can assist with cleaning up your social networks.
■**SEO and management** - with search engine optimization, corporate online reputation management firms will work to mitigate negative customer feedback and work to ensure that Internet users won't only find you but will the information they find on you in the search results will be positive, authentic and useful.
■**Blogs** are a good way to get your brand out there on the web. Apart from showing up on your SERPs and publishing positive information about your brand, blogging attracts

more traffic than static websites which helps with your reputation.

Protect your Online Presence

Each reputation management campaign requires a tailored approach to your particular brand strategy. Changing the public's perception of your particular business is going to take money, effort and time which you may not have. The best way to steer clear of these negative influences is to hire professionals who have the skills to protect your brands reputation. They work to get rid of negativity surrounding your brand before it gets out of hand.

Online reputation management isn't just another passing marketing gimmick. It is a critical part for protecting your brand's reputation. It will decrease the chances of your good online reputation being tarnished and present your business from landing up in the Internet Graveyard.

Visual Online Reputation Management

The visual online representation (VORM) is a key component to a company's online reputation. The images that arise when a company is searched can either highlight the strengths of the company or might be showcasing possible weaknesses in the company.

Additionally without a strong online presence, when searched, a particular company may not show up at all preventing potential customers and possibility pointing them to a competitor that does show up.

⇧ **VORM** ⇧

The best ways to manage online visual reputations are to, first, search and monitor what images are currently available. This will allow companies to gauge what, if any, presence they are portraying. The next step is to gather as much virtual real estate as possible so that the company can be in control of as much of their online presence as possible.

Having as many websites and social media platforms as possible, including photo sharing websites, Facebook, twitter, etc. allows a company to control what visual media gets attached to their name across a broad spectrum. The more virtual real estate a company has, the more likely a potential consumer will come across a company controlled page rather than a random website.

So, go ahead and search for your name. If you don't see pictures associated with you in the search results, deal with it! For example, you might see a picture about yourself that shows on your external blog. Go to that blog and change the picture and very soon it will reflect in search results since the search engine showed that picture based on the picture on that blog! Got it? Follow the links and deal with the pictures in sites that the links lead to…

Press Release As A Tool To Enhance Your Online Brand & Reputation

We're competing with people from the day we're born. Competing for our mom's attention, competing at school to be top of the class, competing on the sports field, in relationships and in business...

From the moment we apply for our first job, we have to create a unique, outstanding career brand so that prospective employers can choose our professional skills and accomplishments over other candidates applying for the same job.

A Press Release a Key Part of your Company's Brand (And Executives)

The business market is highly competitive, and if you want to succeed you have to use every tactic in the book to make your business succeed. There is truth in the saying that successful people aren't always the ones with the most talent but rather the best marketed. A press release is a great way to get yourself marketed - to get word out about your business, yourself and your business executives.

There are many excellent online tools such as The PR Toolkit and PitchEngine among others which help you create and distribute a press release for very little money, and sometimes free of charge. Press releases have become awesome tools for distributing content to consumers and the media and they have been known to garner hundreds of incoming links.

PLEASE GET THIS! READ THE MAIN POINT OF THIS ARTICLE BELOW!

Again, creating and distributing press release will help your online reputation. This is especially the case when a local (or national) paper publishes your press releases and even better calls you to interview you about an article. The online version of that article with proper tags and names (e.g., your name) and links to your website will have massive impact on your reputation.

Imagine the impact on Google search engine results, when your name shows up on Los Angeles Times or whatever other forms of media. Online Reputation Management is NOT just about removing negative information about you – instead, it is also about creating positive information about you (or your firm) and having Google go through its process and as a result, showing that positive content on its search engine.

Press release can help you! It is less about Google seeing your press release and more about Google seeing articles about you in major media. So PLEASE read the rest of this article, not to learn about writing a press release, but learn about writing great releases so you can get interviews with the media.

THAT interview can have massive online reputation benefits for you if handled properly. Make sure the media publishes the article in its digital version too so you get great online reputation benefits! Ok, now that you know how writing a great press release can help your online reputation, let's focus on writing great releases!

Short, Punchy Stories to Pique Interest

A press release is a short, punchy story for certain members of the media in order to pique their interest about what is considered as vital information. These press releases contain essential information such as contact information of the person who wrote the release. Of course, for a marketer, the headline is the most important part of the entire press release. Intriguing, mesmerizing and newsworthy, it will be the deciding factor as to whether the press release gets read at all.

When you email your press release to a journalist, remember they are inundated by other emails, so treat the subject line like royalty and make sure it grabs the journalist's attention. Done right, your press release will soon have your cell phone ringing non-stop as news people try to reach you and set up an interview with you about your press release, products and services.

The idea of a press release is to make it similar to a story in your local newspaper. Just Like a standard news story, you'll want to summarize the main news in the first sentence or paragraph and use the body of the press release to answer questions you imagine people want to know about your product and services without being overly promotional. Press releases always end with a short description of the company issuing the release, complete with a call to action.

Affordable Distribution Services

Some marketers want to make use of a press release to get word out about their products and services. But they hold back because they believe they are too costly. Even using an established service doesn't have to break the bank. There are some services however which provide a huge distribution of your press release but which cost quite a bit.

There are other excellent low-cost distribution services which allow you to distribute a press release for well under $100. For a small business, it can be great getting your release on the world wide web and not just on your own website. Use quality distribution channels. Distribution costs money and there is a lot of debate about which press release distribution service is the best. You'll also pay more if you want to add videos and photographs and social media signals etc. PR Web is one of the most profitable of all distribution services because you can add hyperlinks and images free of charge.

Reach your Target Audience through the Media

Before you write a press release, determine who you are targeting and use keywords and phrases in order to have your press release easily located by reporters looking for specific information. To reach your target audience - the media and consumers - you simply have to have a compelling title so as to capture and hold attention. Keep your press release to one page and make sure it is interesting and not like a brash sales pitch.

When you consider that there are thousands of press releases distributed each day by marketers, you begin to see how difficult it can be for your press release and business to stand out in the crowd. Press releases have great impact, and online distribution of press releases has great value for getting the attention of journalists, getting your message to your target audience and getting this specific audience to take action.

Do research. There is plenty of information available on the Internet which will show you how to optimize your press release so that it does get noticed. For instance one of the basic techniques with on page optimization for web content is to use anchor text links. The reason for this is that they add value to your press release and also to the websites you are linking to by helping the search engines see what the link to your website is about. They also increase the probability that someone will click on your link.

Make Sure Your Press Release can be Located

Your Press Release certainly has the opportunity to receive maximum exposure, and there are certain things you can do to maximize its visibility and interest -

•make your headline something worth announcing - even a well optimized heading won't yield results if the topic or headline is boring
•provide the reader with a reason to click through - a direct to consumer release needs more than an announcement of news. You want to provide the reader with an action opportunity such as special offers, podcasts and newsletters etc. Embed links in your press release to relevant resources as well as a call to action.

You've Got the Edge

Optimized press releases help you get ranked in News search engines where millions of visitors are visiting every day. Editors will be contacting you as a source for fresh content based on your optimized press release. Optimized press releases target your audience and build brand awareness with them. As an effective marketing tool, your press release will enjoy heavy traffic from potential clients and you'll soon be looking at results that show you've got the edge over your competitors. The best scenario is when an article about you (or your firm) is written in the digital edition of a major news media – instant

How to Enhance Your Online Reputation in 30 Hours!

Well, follow these guidelines as needed!

Hours 1st and 2nd:

Search Google, Yahoo and Bing top 10 pages based on searching your name, your business name, or any other name that you care about its reputation. Write the name of the link and the position on search engines (e.g. story about my college days on the 3rd page of Google and 7th page of Yahoo).

Hours 3rd and 4th:

Create various alerts on search engines such as Google Alert or Yahoo alert. Also check for alerts about your name on social media in sites such as http://www.socialmention.com.

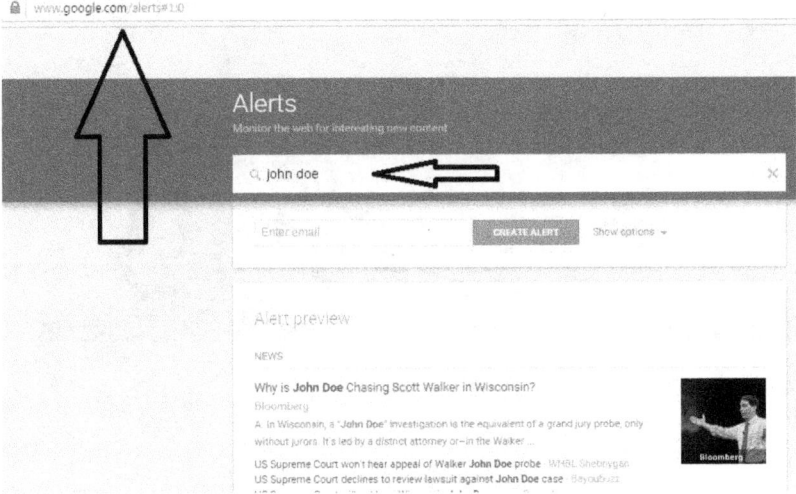

Hours 5th to 15th:

Create as many mini sites as possible about yourself or your business on free sites such as weebly.com. wix.com, wordpress.com, blogger.com and sites.google.com.

Add as much useful and positive content as possible to these sites with great pictures.

Don't forget the primary keywords! If you want to improve the online reputation of "John Doe" then create site name such as http://John-doe.wix.com. Try to use the keyword in site domain name and the title of the site and in few locations in the body of the site content. Here is an example of what I did for myself in one of the sites for the keywords "Koz Khosravani" on free sites.google.com: https://sites.google.com/site/kozkhosravanibio

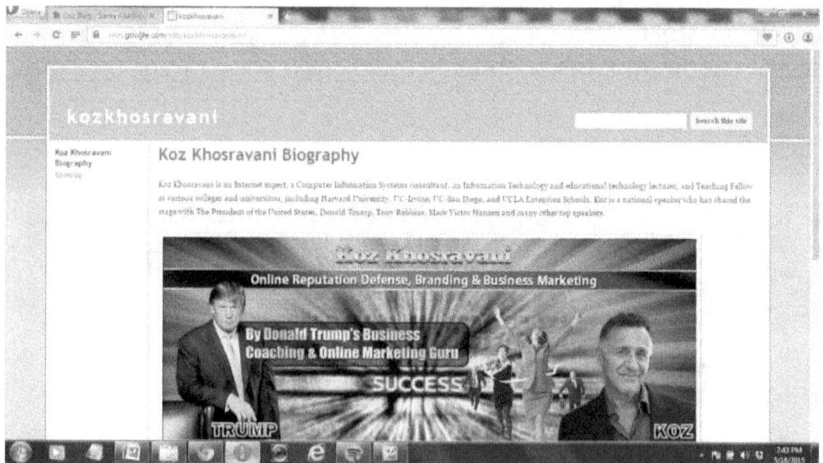

Hours 16th to 20th:

Create as many social sites as possible (i.e. as many social profiles on social sites). So go ahead and use your primary keyword for ORM (e.g. John Doe) to create profiles on Facebook, Twitter, Instagram, LinkedIn, Vimeo, YouTube, Tumblr and other lesser known sites.

Make sure you write great titles, good content, great pictures, etc. Take your time and truly create a great profile. Then, try to connect with as many friends as possible.

Hint: If you created a free Wordpress site in previous hours, you can use it to tie to many social profiles. So when you post a blog post to Wordpress, it will automatically shows on Facebook and many other social sites! Cool! Saves you lots of time!

Hours 21st to 28th:

Ok previous steps allowed us to create many positive online entities that Google can pick up soon.... Now let's locate all search results that are negative in nature!

Contact the webmaster of the site that shows it. Be polite and tell them how it is hurting you and your business. Show them how the information is not accurate or misleading.

Contact whoever wrote it in the first place and see if they are willing to delete it! Be nice and don't get emotional. Don't fight them – it gets worse.

Hire an attorney specializing in online slander to help you. They might be able to trace even anonymous people behind posts and sue them...

If you can't delete the negative items, focus on positive items you created in previous steps and try to get them above the negative entries by being active in the social sites and adding constant content to the free sites that you built!

Hours 29th to 30th:

Review everything. Add more content to the sites that you build. And if you still needed help, contact me. I will do my best to help you. **But I did not write this mini book just to market myself.** I really think that if you follow my simple advice, you can learn a lot and you can see ORM in action! But if you truly needed help or did not have time to do it yourself, visit my site at http://www.KozWealthSystems.com to contact me. Or just call 888-574-1215. Best of luck!

THANK YOU FOR READING! NOW IT IS TIME TO TAKE ACTION. PLEASE UNDERSTAND THAT GETTING EDUCATED IS JUST THE BEGINNING. YOU MUST TAKE ACTION AND IMPLEMENT WHAT YOU LEARNED.

THIS BOOK WAS WRITTEN FOR TOTAL BEGINNERS TO THE FIELD OF APPLIED ONLINE REPUTATION MANAGEMENT. WE HOPE IT OPENED YOUR EYES ABOUT MANY AREAS THAT YOU SHOULD LEARN MORE ABOUT. GOOD LUCK...

PLEASE NOTE THAT WE CANNOT GIVE YOU TAX, LEGAL OR ANY OTHER PROFESSIONAL ADVICE. EVERYTHING HERE WAS EDUCATIONAL IN NATURE BASED ON OUR OWN EXPERIENCES. ALWAYS CONSULT AN ATTORNEY AND TAX PROFESSIONAL IF NEEDED.

About the Author
http://www.KozWealthSystems.com

Koz Khosravani is an Internet expert, a Computer Information Systems consultant, an Information Technology and educational technology lecturer, and Teaching Fellow at various colleges and universities, including Harvard University, UC-Irvine, UC-San Diego, and UCLA Extension Schools.

Koz is a national speaker who has shared the stage with The President of the United States, Donald Trump, Tony Robbins, George Foreman, Lisa Nichols, David Bach, Chris Howard and many other top speakers.

Koz is the only Internet Expert who was invited to be on stage with Donald Trump, Tony Robbins, and others to speak at major wealth Expos in New York and Chicago Convention Centers.

He has been active in the field of Information Technology and education for approximately fifteen years as a software engineer, project manager, educator, trainer, and consultant. He has trained technical employees at various Fortune 500 companies, including Digital Equipment Corporation, Raytheon, Hughes, Edison International, and Boeing (M-Douglas).

His area of specialization includes Internet promotion and marketing, Internet conversions (converting site visitors to buyers and repeat buyers), digital movie editing, digital movie production and post-production, educational technology, e-business security & back-end integration, distributed relational database management systems, wireless technologies, networking, web development, and distributed applications.

Koz designed boot-camp-type fast-track Web Mastering programs for both UCLA and UC-Irvine to benefit those who want to learn about all aspects of website design, construction, and implementation - all in one intense week.

Koz taught a variety of Educational and Instructional Technology courses, including the Internet for Educators, Online Research for Educators, and Advanced Microcomputers in the Classroom (Clear Credential).

He designed and deployed a variety of short business workshops and consulting sessions in the areas of negotiations, communications, business management, MIS, and investments. In addition, he has served on the UCI and UCLA Extension School's advisory committees to develop certificate programs in E-Business and Educational Technology.

Koz created a new program at UCI Extension (2000-2001) entitled "E-Commerce for Entrepreneurs & Small Business Owners". He also taught E-Business Technology overview, E-Business Back-end Integration, and E-Business Security for UCI's Business division. On a lower "system" level, Koz taught VAX-Macro systems programming and Macro-11 at Harvard University.

He has served on the UCLA Alumni Association Board of Directors, UCLA Wooden Athletic Center Board of Governors, UCLA's Executive Vice Chancellor's Academic Planning & Budget Advisory Committee (APBAC), UCLA Academic Senate's Professional School's Restructuring Committees, and UCSA Board of Governors, as well as other educational and social organization's governing boards.